Hal Roach's Rascals: The Our Gang Comedies

A Classic Collection

I. Joseph Hyatt

To purchase books in quantity for fund raising, classroom use or to use as incentives email MovieCollector@aol.com.

Copyright © 2016 I. Joseph Hyatt

All rights reserved.

ISBN: 153744204X
ISBN-13: 978-1537442044

Dedication

To all the people who worked on the films in front of and behind the cameras. To all the people who worked in the offices creating the publicity. To all the people that helped in the distribution and exhibition of this movie. To all the people working today to preserve and make available classic films to the public.

To my wife Mary who has put up with my old movie obsession all these years.

To Dave Lord Heath, Gino Dercola and Roger Robinson for their help in bringing this series of books together with its audience. (A special thank you to Dave and his website "Another Nice Mess." His hard work made a writer's work much easier.)

Thanks for the constant feedback from you, the reader. It makes the series better.

To Mark Eisler and his family and to Cliff Sawyer, just for being a phone call away. To Eric Schultz, Louis Respen, and Edward Heijne for their consistent support.

To the members of the Sons of the Desert, the Laurel and Hardy Appreciation Society, for helping to keep the films of Laurel and Hardy alive.

Thanks to Rick Green for sharing many of his lobby cards, and to Randy Skretvedt, the authority on the work of Laurel and Hardy.

Finally, a big thanks to the Laurel and Hardy Museum in Ulverston, Cumbria, UK for almost 35 years of exhibitions. Marion (Bill's daughter) and Mark (Bill's grandson) continue to operate the museum, now in its larger quarters at the old Roxy Cinema, just behind Ulverston's Coronation Hall. They are two of the most knowledgeable and friendly people, sharing their collection and information with visitors to the town where Stan Laurel was born. Bill Cubin, former mayor and museum founder, would have been proud of how the museum grew.

Acknowledgements

Our Gang comedies are available on DVD wherever you buy your movies and books.

Many of the silent films and four of the sound shorts are in the public domain and have been released to the home market in copies that vary from low quality to very good copies. Read the on-line reviews carefully before you purchase any of these titles. While the films are always good fun to watch, the quality of the image will impact your enjoyment of the movies. Spend a few dollars more and try to get the best versions out there. You will enjoy them more.

A full set of the Hal Roach sound shorts are distributed for the home market by Vivendi Entertainment. This set includes the classic silent short "Dog Heaven."

The later M-G-M shorts (post Hal Roach) are available through Warner Home Video as a full set only. Hal Roach's "General Spanky" is available from Warners Home Video as single DVD. These are a part of the Warner Archive series, and are not stocked items but are made on demand when ordered.

Introduction

For many "old time" movie fans that grew up in the sixties and seventies, television gave us our first exposure to classic films. In a day before video tape recorders, cable, streaming, DVD, Blu-ray, and computers we considered ourselves lucky when one of our favorite movies was broadcast. With the exception of the CBS annual broadcast of "The Wizard of Oz" and stations such as New York's WOR that ran one movie (Million Dollar Movie) eleven times a week, an average movie would probably air twice in a five-year period.

To our delight, short subjects like "The Little Rascals," "The Three Stooges," and "Laurel and Hardy" aired almost daily. These shorts were a very important part of our childhood. Since we couldn't own a copy of the film as you can today, many of us tried to "capture" a bit of the emotions we felt by buying magazines, comics, toys, photos, and records with our favorite movie personalities. Sound tracks were recorded on our reel-to-reel audio tape recorders. Some of us even had a family home movie projector where you could buy a few minutes of older films and cartoons in 8mm silent (later sound) editions for a reasonable price (if we saved up our money and dad let us use the family projector). For most of us, a more professional film gauge was just an expensive dream.

Today "collectables" like lobby cards, photos, and other movie memorabilia are very expensive. Back in the 1960's and earlier theaters and movie distributors would recycle posters, photos and movie campaign books until the films reached the end of their theatrical showings. Then these paper items would be disposed of. The suppliers (like National Cinema Service) either threw them out or gave these mementoes to anyone who would clear their warehouse.

Stores like Marc Ricci's Memory Shop in New York City and many more acquired much of this material by the truckload. Before these items were considered collectable (or even worthy of preservation) we could purchase some of these photos, lobby cards, and posters between $1 - $7 each in these stores, or through mail order. Normally 11" x 14" in size, most lobby cards came in sets of eight.

Now many full size movie posters sell in the 5 and 6 figures range. Pre-1940 material is the most expensive, since many of the paper items were donated (and recycled) for the war effort. Today it takes a collector with "deep pockets" to afford some of the original material.

Black and white and duo-tone cards have been presented here in color, as they should be, to enhance the details and artwork on the cards. Sadly, age in some cases has turned the paper of the color tinted and black and white images into a light brown. With color cards, some color fading is to be expected. Remember that much of this material is close to 90 years old. The color differences you might notice in many cards for the same movies are because collections were built from various sources at various times. Rarely today is a full set offered for sale.

Archives and movie studios are now actively restoring and preserving the advertising materials that still exist today. Auction houses sell this material at a premium price.

I hope that after seeing the original publicity materials for these films it will encourage you to seek out the movies. Due to the scarcity of original material, not all of the Our Gang films are represented in this book. I hope the following reproductions of lobby cards, posters, and trade magazine ads will meet with your approval.

I. Joseph Hyatt
September 3, 2016

"Our Gang" Lobby Cards
The silent Hal Roach Pathecomedy releases:

Young Sherlocks

The Big Show

Boy to Board

Stage Fright

Tire Trouble

Big Business

Buccaneers

Every Man for Himself

Fast Company

"OUR GANG" COMEDY

Hotel McSwigger - Where a dime's worth of boiled potatoes costs $5.

Hal Roach presents His Rascals in

FAST COMPANY

Pathécomedy

"OUR GANG" COMEDY

Farina - Sleeps eight hours - Plays eight hours - Eats eight hours

Hal Roach presents His Rascals in

FAST COMPANY

Pathécomedy

The Love Bug

One Wild Ride

Buried Treasure

Monkey Business

War Feathers

The Glorious Forth

Bring Home the Turkey

Playin' Hookey

The Smile Wins

"Our Gang" Lobby Cards
The Silent Hal Roach Metro-Goldwyn-Mayer releases:

Yale vs. Harvard

Growing Pains

The Ol' Gray Hoss

Wiggle Your Ears

Fast Freight

HAL ROACH *presents*
OUR GANG *in* **FAST FREIGHT**

HAL ROACH *presents*
OUR GANG *in* **FAST FREIGHT**

Little Mother

Saturday's Lesson

"Our Gang" Lobby cards
The sound Hal Roach
Metro-Goldwyn-Mayer
releases:

Boxing Gloves

Pups Is Pups

Teacher's Pet

Birthday Blues

Beginner's Luck

Divot Diggers

? **What's Hal Roach got up his sleeve now! Listen, it's a swell idea!**

DICKIE MOORE

WHEEZER   STYMIE

8 ALL STAR "OUR GANG" COMEDIES

Here's how Hal Roach celebrates the 10th Anniversary of "Our Gang"

"SPANKY" steals the show!

That's what the N. Y. American said! That's what critics and public everywhere say about "Spanky"!

BOUNCY

PETE

When we say "*All Star*" we mean it! Every member of the new "Our Gang" is hand-picked for name value! Dickie Moore for example has appeared in eight feature pictures, and has an important part in Marlene Dietrich's next film. Exhibitors tell us that patrons watch for each appearance of "Spanky" the child wonder. "Our Gang" takes a new lease on life at their 10th Anniversary. You'll approve of Hal Roach's improvements!

1932

Hal Roach's "Our Gang" feature-length movie "General Spanky"

General Spanky

General Spanky

The General's heart is softened by Spanky's plea for the prisoner.

A Metro-Goldwyn-Mayer RELEASE

General Spanky

"A salute, to the bravest little soldier of them all!"

A Metro-Goldwyn-Mayer RELEASE

General Spanky

Little did they know the shadow of disaster would fall across their happiness.

A Metro Goldwyn Mayer RELEASE

COUNTRY OF ORIGIN U. S. A.

General Spanky

"We three must stick together!"

A Metro Goldwyn Mayer RELEASE

COUNTRY OF ORIGIN U. S. A.

General Spanky

"I make you two members of my troops!"

A Metro Goldwyn Mayer RELEASE

COUNTRY OF ORIGIN U. S. A.

General Spanky

"Always remember—I love you!"

A Metro Goldwyn Mayer RELEASE

COUNTRY OF ORIGIN U. S. A.

"Our Gang" Posters
The silent Hal Roach Pathecomedy releases:

The Big Show

The Cobbler

The Champeen

Tire Trouble

Sunday Calm

Derby Day

Bring Home the Turkey

The Fourth Alarm

Baby Brother

Olympic Games

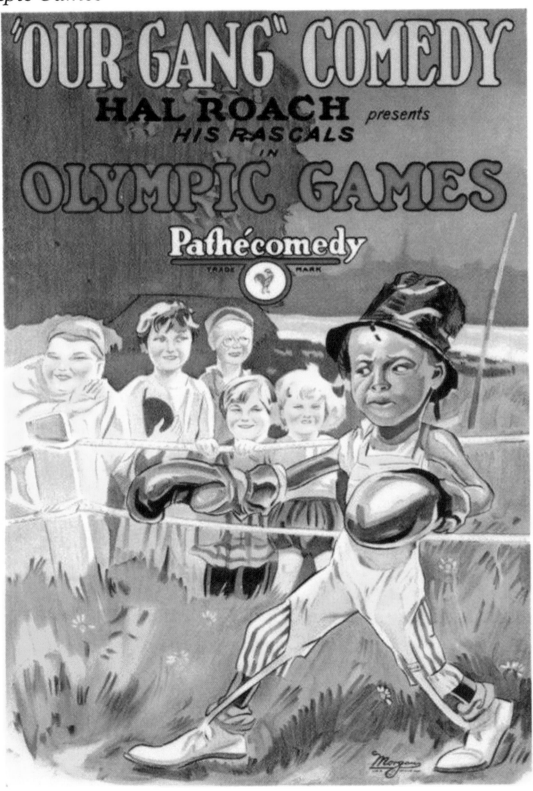

"Our Gang" Posters The sound Hal Roach Metro-Goldwyn Mayer releases:

Love Business

School Begins

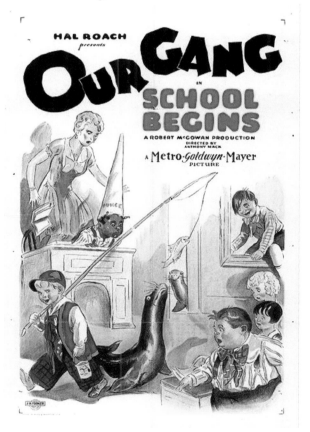

Free Wheeling

The Kid from Borneo

Wild Poses

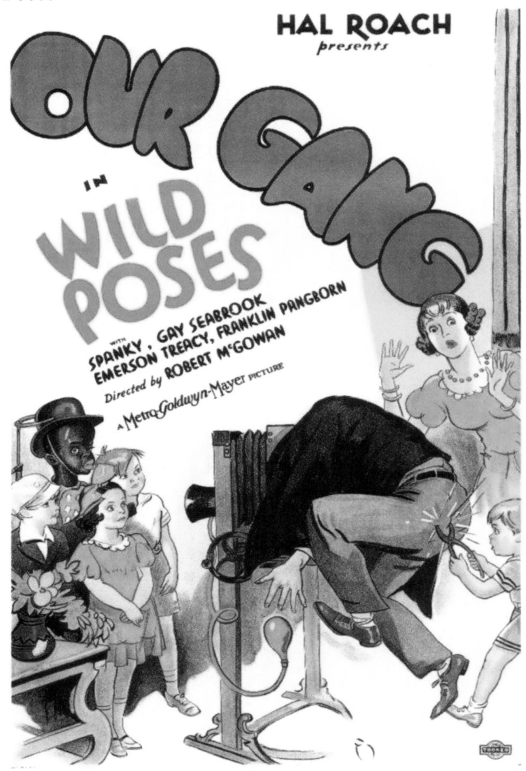

Hi-Neighbor!

The First Round-up

Second Childhood

Pay as You Exit

Three Smart Boys

Three Men in a Tub

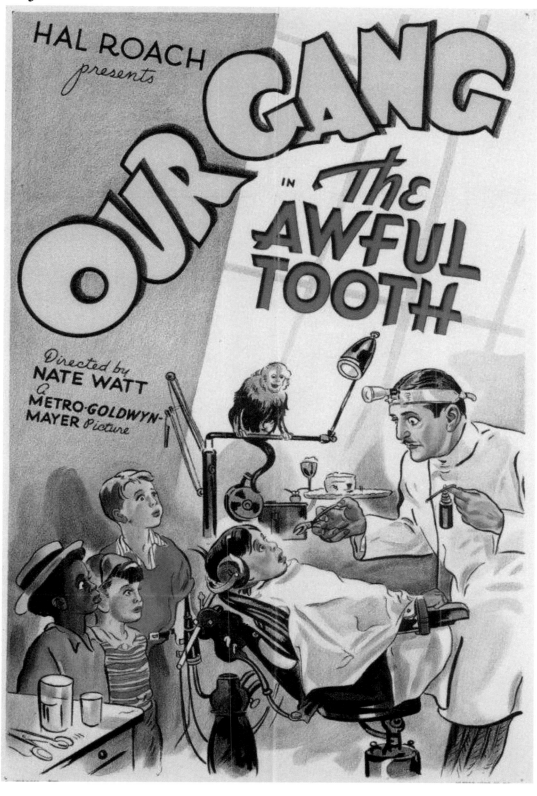

"Our Gang" Posters The Metro-Goldwyn Mayer releases:

Clown Princes

Tiny Troubles

Dog Daze

Alfalfa's Double

Going to Press

Come Back Miss Pipps

Captain Spanky's Show Boat

Joy Scouts

Baby Blues

Goin' Fishin'

Ye Olde Minstrels

"Our Gang"
A collection of trade advertisements:

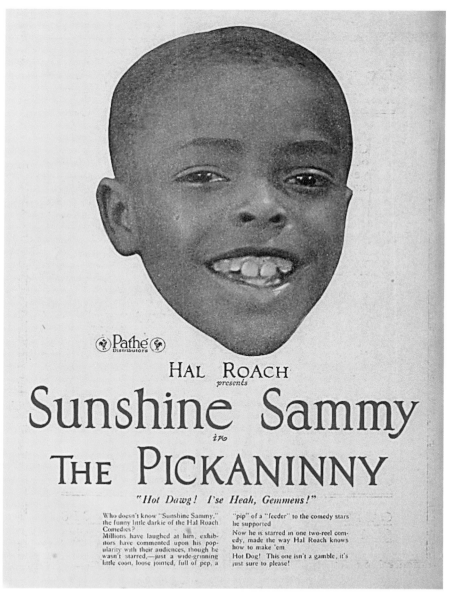

Ernie "Sunshine Sammy" Morrison in a pre-Our Gang comedy from 1922. He was a star before joining the gang.

"The hit of the bill!"—*N. Y. Herald*

Hal Roach *presents*

Our Gang Comedies

Two parts

The first "Our Gang" comedy, "One Terrible Day," was a riot at the Rivoli in New York.

The audience fairly screamed with joy; it got weak with laughter!

> *"The best thing on the Rivoli Theatre program* this week," says the N. Y. Post, "is the funniest comedy shown for some time, 'One Terrible Day,' bringing forth screams of laughter."

> *"The outstanding hit of the bill* at the Rivoli," says the N. Y. Herald, "is a rollicking Pathe comedy, 'One Terrible Day.'"

Play "Our Gang" comedies for more laughter, maximum entertainment, and thoroughly satisfied audiences.

Pathépicture
TRADE MARK

1922

HAL ROACH *presents*

Our Gang Comedies

Two parts each

"FARINA"

"If you have never shown these comedies you have something to live for!"

"If you have never used this comedy you have something to live for."—Mrs. W. M. Kimbro, Greenland, Greensboro, Ga. (Ex. Herald).

The audience just sits up and screams!

"These kid comedies are the cream. The audience just sits up and screams."—L. B. Worth, Gayety, Ft. Worth, Tex. (Ex. Herald).

100 Per cent

"Young Sherlocks is a 100 per cent comedy."— Henry Sanbert, Fad, Fairfax, S. D.

"Great. Our Gang Comedies are 100 per cent." —Jas. D. Kennedy, Apollo, Indianapolis, Ind. (Ex.-Herald).

Simply fine

"Pathe is to be congratulated on these comedies. They're simply fine." Clean," funny comedies which please old and young."—H. G. Sweet, Royal, Royal Center, Ind. (Ex.-Herald).

Full of laughs

"These comedies are very good and full of laughs."—J. W. Creamer, Strand, Chillicothe, Mo. (Ex. Herald).

As good as one could want

"As good as one could want." They please both kids and grownups."—Ray Dowling, Zark, Zark, Ala. (Ex. Herald).

Pathécomedy

TRADE MARK

1923

Hal Roach *presents*

Our Gang Comedies

Two Parts

Less than a year ago the first "Our Gang" comedy was released.

It is believed that today these unique comedies have a wider distribution than any comedies of the same length now produced.

Hal Roach hit upon a great idea. He developed it with striking originality and skill.

The very numerous enthusiastic comments from exhibitors published in the trade papers attest the really amazing popularity of these delightful comedies.

Pathe is pleased to announce a new series of these comedies from Mr. Roach, with "Micky," "Sunshine Sammy," "Farina," "Jackie," the "Tough Kid" and all the rest of the laughable urchins.

13—Sold in Series of Six.

Pathécomedy
TRADE MARK

1923

1924

Hal Roach presents

"Our Gang" Comedies

Two parts

They've brought you weekly, throughout the past year the best of gifts,—good business, happy patrons, thousands of laughs.

They will deliver to you during 1924 the same, but in even greater measure,—heaping full and running over.

The exhibitor who books "Our Gang" comedies is *sure* of a Happy New Year.

Pathécomedy

1924

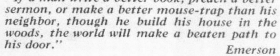

Pathé
Season 1924-1925

Section N° 2
Two Reel
Comedies

Section N° 5
will appear in
this magazine
next week

Hal Roach
"Our Gang" Comedies
Two Reels · One Series of 12

*"If a man write a better book, preach a better
sermon, or make a better mouse-trap than his
neighbor, though he build his house in the
woods, the world will make a beaten path to
his door."*

Emerson

MANY producers had tried to make pictures with all-child casts.
No such pictures were ever successful before Hal Roach made
his first "Our Gang" comedy. The success of these inimitable child comedies was immediate. Their quality was
and is outstanding. No wonder that they are the most
praised, most widely booked two reel comedies of the day

The world has made a beaten path
to the door of Hal Roach and his
"Our Gang" comedies; for he has
made "something better."

10,289 Exhibitors were
playing these Comedies
last year

Pathécomedy

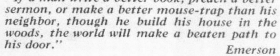

1924

Ever see a little but powerful
pleasure car drag a big truck out
of the mud?
That's what an Our Gang Comedy
will do for your show when you've
got anything but the very biggest
feature on it!

Hal Roach presents

Boys Will Be Joys

an

Our Gang Comedy

a Two Reel

Tell them about it!

F. Richard Jones, Supervising Director

Pathécomedy
TRADE MARK

1925

Hal Roach *presents*

Official Officers

a Two Reel

Our Gang Comedy

Don't show it if you love melancholy

F. Richard Jones, Supervising Director

TRADE MARK

1925

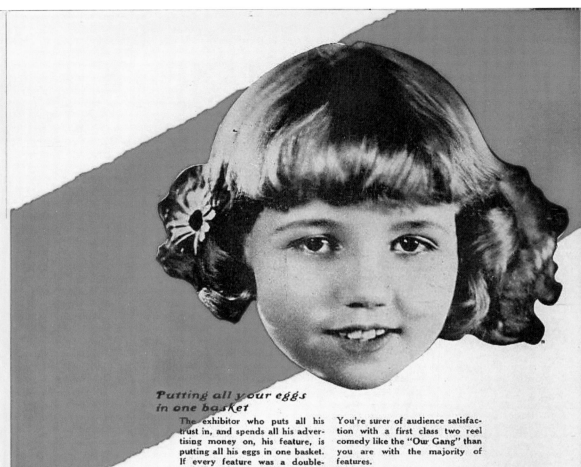

Putting all your eggs in one basket

The exhibitor who puts all his trust in, and spends all his advertising money on, his feature, is putting all his eggs in one basket. If every feature was a double-dyed knockout there might be some excuse. But they aren't and never will be.

You're surer of audience satisfaction with a first class two reel comedy like the "Our Gang" than you are with the majority of features.

In the name of good business, then, why keep them a secret?

Hal Roach *presents*

Mary, Queen of Tots

a Two Reel

Our Gang Comedy

The wonderful little kids in one of their biggest laughs

F. Richard Jones, Supervising Director

Pathécomedy

TRADE ⬡ MARK

1925

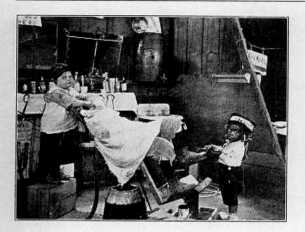

Start An "OUR GANG" Day

IT WOULD be a relatively simple procedure to instigate an "Our Gang" Week in your town, independently of any similar action to be taken up nationally. The advantages to be derived therefrom are not to be denied. Good will and a well satisfied patronage is one direct result from any stunt of this sort. It brings your theatre far out into the limelight.

HOW TO BEGIN

Enlist the services of your local troop of Boy Scouts in a campaign to organize an "Our Gang" club. The Boy Scouts will be glad to cooperate because it will also give them an opportunity to increase their enlistments. Allow the use of your theatre one morning each week for about a month before the celebration for the purposes of organizing. Interest several well known men to help in the organization of these clubs, whose purposes will be similar to those of the Boy Scouts.

LAY OUT ACTIVITIES PROGRAM

Make your plans for the celebration week to include a "father and son" baseball game or a golf tournament, or some similar sport, depending upon the relative popularity in your community.

Include in this program of sports everything that is made

Great Opportunity for a Real Community Picnic Day

possible by the advantages enjoyed by your community; swimming meets, marble shooting contest, harmonica contest and so on.

NON-ATHLETIC PROGRAM

To those for whom athletic events have little call, you can arrange an essay contest to be run in the leading newspaper of your town. Themes should be along ideas of betterment for youngsters, more understanding between young and old, and such. It might also prove very interesting to

Beech-Nut Fruit Drops are going to play a prominent role in the exploitation of "Our Gang." If you think that a number of sample packages for distribution on "Our Gang" Day will help, make your request to Exhibitors Trade Review.

get some opinions from the successful men of the town concerning their youthful activities, and whether or no they believe that the gang spirit that exists in all young boys is or is not advantageous to the character building of the young ones.

ASK DAD

You might put direct questions to mothers and fathers asking whether they would punish their boy if he were to engage in a "grudge" fight occasionally; whether they object to their young daughters hob-nobbing with the boys; whether they believe that allowing boys and girls to play together does not have its beneficial results in toning down the boy and adding a manly spirit of fair play to the girl.

SKIP MATINEE SHOWING

For a grand finale, so far as your theatre is concerned, keep it closed during the time you usually give your matinee performances on the day when all the athletic contests are being held. Arrange to have that day fall on the afternoon that you usually do your slowest business, and you will more than make up the loss by two full houses that night. Advertise the fact well that you are keeping the house closed for just that reason, and that will even tend to get a better showing at the contests.

1925

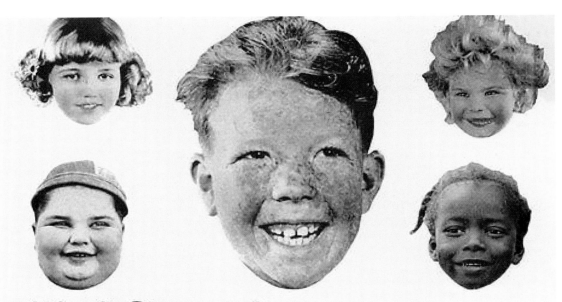

Hal Roach presents

"Our Gang" in

"Good Cheer" Two Reels

A snow picture, the Gang's first, with the inimitable Gang at the bottom of all the fun and all the drifts.

Over ten thousand exhibitors have found that when they play a Gang comedy and tell their people they've got it, *it will outdraw the feature.*

This remarkable crew of kids is advertised on more marquees and in more newspaper advertising than probably any short comedies ever made.

Every month is Laugh Month if you play "Our Gang."

Directed by
ROBERT McGOWAN

Supervising Director
F. RICHARD JONES

Pathécomedy
TRADE MARK

RELEASED
JANUARY 10TH

January Laugh Month 1926

1926

HAL ROACH

presents

"OUR GANG"

in

"Thundering Fleas"

22% of *all* replies from exhibitors in the May questionnaire of Exhibitors Review name Our Gang Comedies as their biggest money-maker.

Each month has seen Our Gang consistently at the top,—a superb record.

"One Wild Ride" At McVickers Theatre, Chicago

"The comedy was cause for such uproar as might betoken the signing of an armistice . . . The women scream and the children simply cease to breathe."

—Service in Exhibitors Herald

"Thundering Fleas" is an absolute knockout!

Directed by
Robert McGowan

F. Richard Jones,
Supervising Director

1926

HAL ROACH
presents
OUR GANG
COMEDIES

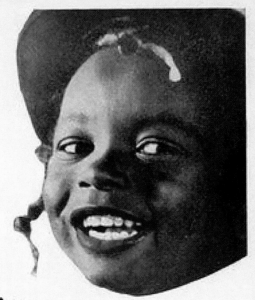

Wouldn't you be lucky

if only one half of the features you
show had *half* of the box office value
of the "Gangs?"

Directed by Robert McGowan
F. Richard Jones, Supervising Director

Pathécomedy
TRADE MARK

1927

TOUCHDOWN
FOR
M·G·M'S
"OUR GANG"

Three Cheers (and more) for Hal Roach!

HAVE you seen
"YALE" vs. Harvard" (dunt esk!)
IT'S a pleasure to add this
WONDERFUL "Our Gang" comedy
TO M·G·M's Big-Time program.
THE next Hal Roach "Our Gang"
IS "The Old Wallop," and it's
POSITIVELY those kids' best yet!
M·G·M Shorts are certainly *there!*

THOSE M·G·M SHORTS!
(really the best!)

HAL ROACH COMEDIES
10 OUR GANG
10 MAX DAVIDSON
10 CHARLEY CHASE
10 ALL-STAR

M·G·M NEWS
Twice Weekly—The World's Spotlight

M·G·M GREAT EVENTS
Six Entirely in Technicolor

M·G·M ODDITIES
26 produced all over the world
by UFA

METRO-GOLDWYN-MAYER

JUNIOR FEATURES
The Cream of Wit

1927

QUICK!

OUR GANG in
SMALL TALK
and 2 more

Get out the pen!
OUR GANG
All-Talking
Comedies

HURRY!

LAUREL-HARDY in
THEIR LAST WORD
and 2 more

Grab 'em!
LAUREL-
HARDY
All-Talking
Comedies

FAST!

CHARLIE CHASE in
THE BIG SQUAWK
and 2 more

ROACH ALL-STARS in
NOISY NEIGHBORS
and 2 more

Act now!
CHARLIE
CHASE
All-Talking
Comedies

HAL ROACH'S
ALL-TALKING
(Victor Recording)
COMEDIES NOW READY!

Another milestone in the history of Talking Pictures. Imagine the thrill of hearing Farina, Fatty Joe Cobb and the rest of the Gang! Think how your patrons will flock to hear the screamingly funny Laurel-Hardy and Charlie Chase. Celebrated figures! And now they talk! Here are the funniest, cleverest, ALL-DIALOGUE pictures that can be had. Don't lose a minute. Book them now!

Starting May 4th
ONE A WEEK
M-G-M

1927 – Notice the "sound" related titles. Laurel and Hardy never made a film called "Their Last Word."

Hal Roach, *producer, and* R. F. McGowan, *director,* of "Our Gang" Comedies—

Say:

"We have used many Bell & Howell professional motion picture cameras in the past 15 years in making our comedy productions, and have used them *exclusively* for 'Our Gang' features. The great adaptability and precision of these machines under the most exacting professional requirements, explain to us, in a great measure, the tremendous success you have had with your Filmo cameras and equipment."

THERE'S a thrill in making your own movies. Living pictures of your old folks—the children—your pets and hobbies—are bits of your life today that will prove priceless possessions later on. But personal movies will only prove as good as the camera and equipment used to produce them.

So start right! Avoid disappointment and loss of pictures that can never be re-

Filmo 75

The beautiful pocket size Filmo 75 is in every respect a fitting companion to the larger Filmo 70. Combining lightness with great strength and rigidity it is especially suitable for field, travel and outdoor sports. Filmo 75 is furnished in three rich colors: Walnut Brown, Ebony Black and Silver Birch. Price $120, including case.

taken by using a dependable Bell & Howell Filmo Camera. It will always give you the truly professional results you have a right to expect, because Filmo is really professional equipment designed for personal use.

With Filmo, anyone can make perfect home movies—pictures of the quality demanded by Hal Roach and other famous producers. It's easier than taking snapshots. Merely look through the "spy-glass" viewfinder, press the button and "What you see, you get"—every time!

Remember that these famous Filmo "home movie" cameras are made with the same watch-like precision that characterizes the wonderful Bell & Howell professional studio cameras costing up to $5000—used for the past 22 years in producing a majority of the photoplays shown in "first-run" theaters.

For black and white pictures, Filmo cameras use Eastman Safety Film (16mm.)—in the yellow box—both regular and panchromatic—obtainable at practically all dealers handling cameras and supplies. Filmo Cameras and Filmo Projectors are adaptable, under license

from Eastman Kodak Company, for use of Eastman Kodacolor film for home movies in full color. Cost of film covers developing and return, postpaid, within the country where processed, ready to show at home or anywhere.

See a nearby dealer for complete Filmo demonstration, or write for illustrated, descriptive movie booklet, "What You See, You Get."

Filmo 70

The original and most highly perfected automatic personal movie camera ever produced. Price $180, including case. Other models for making slow-motion movies.

BELL & HOWELL

BELL & HOWELL CO., Dept. F1, 1803 Larchmont Ave., CHICAGO, ILL. • NEW YORK • HOLLYWOOD • LONDON (B. & H. Co., Ltd.) • Established 1907

1933

THELMA TODD
PATSY KELLY

Exhibitors tell us they have become the female Laurel-Hardy team! Your public will like these gay, giddy gals more than ever in their new routine.

CHARLIE CHASE

A welcome addition to any program, because the Charlie Chase comedy has long proved itself a consistently likable fun film. An established marquee name!

IRVIN S. COBB

The first Irvin S. Cobb comedies have definitely confirmed the showmanship inspiration of Hal Roach. The chuckling personality of America's idol is on the screen!

OUR GANG

It has been an achievement in picture making to successfully present these juvenile stars during so many years. The public loves them, and Spanky and his Gang go merrily on!

1934

THEY PLAY
RINGS AROUND
ALL OTHER
COMEDY SHORTS!

1934

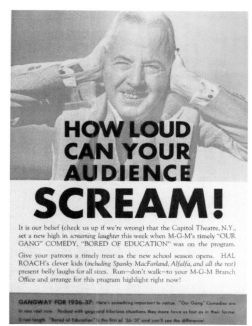

HOW LOUD CAN YOUR AUDIENCE SCREAM!

It is our belief (check us up if we're wrong) that the Capitol Theatre, N.Y., set a new high in *screaming laughter* this week when M-G-M's timely "OUR GANG" COMEDY, "BORED OF EDUCATION" was on the program.

Give your patrons a timely treat as the new school season opens. HAL ROACH's clever kids (*including Spanky MacFarland, Alfalfa, and all the rest*) present belly laughs for all sizes. Run—don't walk—to your M-G-M Branch Office and arrange for this program highlight right now!

GANGWAY FOR 1936-37: Here's something important to notice. "Our Gang" Comedies are in one reel now. Packed with gags and hilarious situations they move twice as fast as in their former 2-reel length. "Bored of Education" is the first of '36-37 and you'll see the difference!

1936

Thank Mr. and Mrs. MacFarland for *this* SHORT SUBJECT!

Timed to capitalize on the Amateur Night craze . . . . . And the first of the new showmanship shorts from Hal Roach studios for M-G-M.

LAUREL-HARDY—CHARLEY CHASE—
TODD-KELLY—OUR GANG

1935

Behind the Scenes

Telling Tales Out of School

Here's a recent edition of "Our Gang," gathered around the same Mrs. Fern Carter who has taught the youngsters ever since the series started 15 years ago. You'll recognize Darla Hood, Spanky McFarland, Buckwheat, Alfalfa and the others

IF "SPANKY" McFARLAND, Hal Roach's "million dollar baby," has his way about it, he is going to desert his film career and do nothing but go to school from now on. This decision, in view of the fact that his boss only recently put Spanky under a new seven-year contract, and coming as it did right out of a clear sky, should have had all the devastating effect of a bombshell exploding in the lap of the studio officials. But strangely enough, it didn't.

Spanky's momentous announcement was made on "location" while the last few scenes of *General Spanky* were being filmed. The babystar made it directly in front of the calm and gentle-faced woman by whose side we happened to be sitting and about whom we shall have more to say shortly.

"I'll be awful glad when school starts, Mis' Carter," Spanky said seriously. "It's more fun than all this." He waved a chubby arm toward a spot not far away where men were busy with cameras and lights. "I think I'll go to school all the time and never quit going. Alfalfa says the same thing. Alfalfa says this year he's going to be a whiz—I mean, Mis' Carter, he says he's going to be real extra good in 'rithmetic—can he do that, Mis' Carter?"

Mrs. Fern Carter, who, by the way, has two children of her own and knows child psychology as few women know it, smiled and drew the worried Spanky to her.

"If he studies hard, he will, Spanky," she said in her soft voice. "And you will, too." Her vigilant eyes caught sight of "Buckwheat" Thomas running about as fast as his little legs would carry him.

Mrs. Carter drew Spanky closer.

"Do me a favor, will you please?" she whispered. "Tell Buckwheat that I think it is time for him to take his rest."

"Yes, ma'am, Mis' Carter," Spanky promised and walked away to carry out her order.

We watched as Buckwheat glanced our way. We saw him a moment later stretch out in the cool shade of a nearby tree. He was smiling as you see him smile in *Our Gang Comedies.* There was no sign of resentment on his face or in any of his actions because a sudden halt had been called in his play. He seemed to take it for granted that Mrs. Carter knew what was best for him and accepted her request like a good soldier. Buckwheat is only four years old.

1935

"The Personality Kid," SPANKY McFARLAND

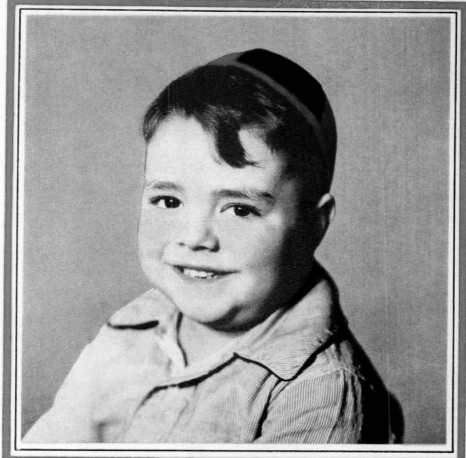

If this turns out the way Hal Roach thinks it will, you've got a new electric light name to challenge *any* existing juvenile star. Good as he was in those merry short subjects Spanky McFarland's got a lot of talent and winsomeness that can only be brought out fully in a full-length feature with character building and story construction. In putting Spanky into a big feature production Mr. Roach really follows the logical development of this grand youngster with audiences and showmen. The deciding factor was Spanky's personal appearance tour when he literally wowed them! So here's his feature debut and it's getting every chance in the way of production, etc. It's a swell comedy built around the Civil War period and a Big role for the little fellow!

SPANKY McFARLAND AND ALL-STAR CAST
in "GENERAL SPANKY"
Director, Fred Newmeyer

1936

OF COURSE SPANKY will continue to star in "Our Gang" comedies now being made by as spry a troupe of youngsters as ever gathered under the Klieg lights. The "Our Gang" Comedies are in 1-reel each now and definitely a bright spot on any program.

ALFALFA! Certainly, there he is in the photo above, second from the right. It sure had to be *trick* photography to remove his freckles from the photograph and to re-arrange those eyes! But on the screen he's got all those things that make folks chuckle and a weirder voice than ever!

NATURALLY Hal Roach will continue to make "Our Gang" Comedies in single reels in addition to his new Feature Production enterprise. The public just wouldn't stand for a discontinuance of "Our Gang". Might as well abolish baseball!

"OUR GANG FOLLIES OF 1937" The first one was such a joy that it's good business all around to have another in the new season. Based on the experience with last season's Gang Follies, they've developed some new Gang gags that are positively marvelous. Wait!

Certainly, in addition to his FEATURES, there will be
12 HAL ROACH-OUR GANG COMEDIES
in One Reel Each

1936

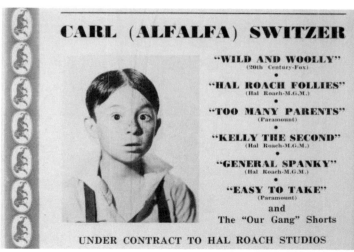

1938

1942

"Little Rascals"

Monogram re-issue stock posters/cards

Bored of Education

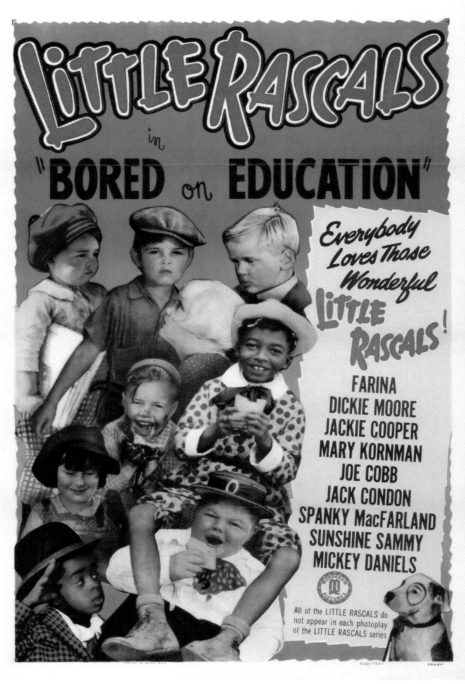

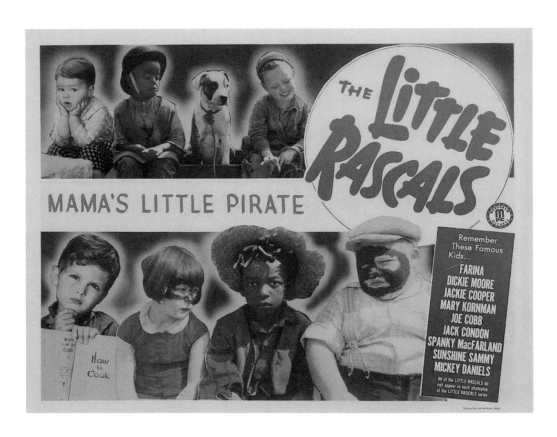

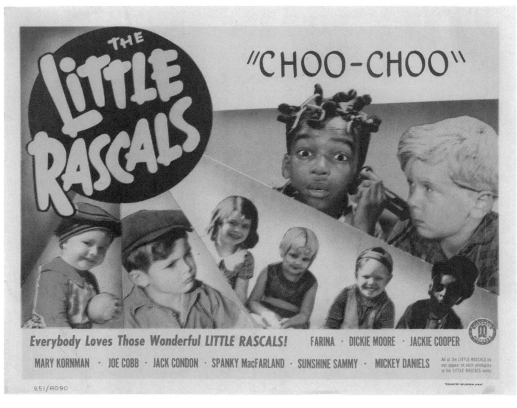

"Little Rascals Varieties"

"Little Rascals Varieties" was a compilation feature-film for theatrical release in 1959. It is made up of four "Our Gang" shorts: "Our Gang Follies of 1936," "The Pinch Singer," "Reunion in Rhythm," and "Our Gang Follies of 1938".

Little Rascals Varieties

Paint Toys from 1934?

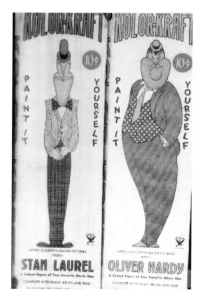

Autographs:

Jackie Lynn

Gordon "Porky" Lee

Tommy "Butch" Bond

Dorothy "Echo" DeBorba

Doorothy "Echo" DeBorba, Jackie Cooper, and Mary Ann Jackson

George "Spanky" McFarland

Mary, Jackie, Mickey, Farina, Joe and Pineapple.
Original 1924 "Our Gang Comedies"

Eugene "Pineapple" Jackson

Jay R. Smith

Priscilla Montgomery

Mildred Kornman

ABOUT THE AUTHOR

I. Joseph Hyatt is an entertainment archeologist. A member of the Sons of the Desert, the Laurel and Hardy Appreciation Society, Hyatt's articles have been printed internationally. Traveling across the US, and drawing on many collections, including his own, he brings back past eras with words and photographs.

His first book, "Stan Laurel's Valet - The Jimmy Murphy Story" was based on his close friendship with Jimmy Murphy. While a biography of one of the world's most entertaining valets, it's focus includes the 1940-42 US theatrical tours of Laurel and Hardy.

"Life and Death of a Movie Theater" tells the story of a small town theater and its competition from the depression through the war years, the television years and through to the current day.

He has also written "Hollywood Victory Caravan" which describes the USA's largest bond tour during the war years. Rare private home movie frames capture and recreate the entire show. Travel with the troupe to all 12 cities. Extra information includes the Mexico pre-show and the San Francisco post-show. Souvenir programs from Bob Hope, Oliver Hardy and Charles Boyer are reproduced along with ticket stubs, crew badges, advertising and publicity photos. Stars include (in alphabetical order) Desi Arnaz, Joan Blondell, Joan Bennett, Charles Boyer, James Cagney, Claudette Colbert, Jerry Colonna, Bing Crosby, Olivia de Havilland, Cary Grant, Charlotte Greenwood, Bob Hope (as Master of Ceremonies), Bert Lahr, Frances Langford, Stan Laurel and Oliver Hardy, Groucho Marx, Frank McHugh, Ray Middleton, Merle Oberon, Pat O'Brien, Eleanor Powell, Rise Stevens, and many more! Available in Color or Black and White editions.

Other books by I. Joseph Hyatt:
The East Side Comedies 1940-1945
Movie Publicity Showcase Volume 1: Laurel and Hardy in "Swiss Miss"
Movie Publicity Showcase Volume 2: Laurel and Hardy in "Saps at Sea"
Movie Publicity Showcase Volume 3: Oliver Hardy and Harry Langdon in "Zenobia"
Movie Publicity Showcase Volume 4: Laurel and Hardy in "The Flying Deuces" & "Utopia"
Movie Publicity Showcase Volume 5: Laurel and Hardy in "Sons of the Desert"
Movie Publicity Showcase Volume 6: Laurel and Hardy in "Thicker Than Water" and other short subjects
Movie Publicity Showcase Volume 7: Laurel and Hardy in "Our Relations"
Movie Publicity Showcase Volume 8: Laurel and Hardy in "Any Old Port" and other short subjects
Movie Publicity Showcase Volume 9: Laurel and Hardy in "Pack Up Your Troubles"
Movie Publicity Showcase Volume 10: Laurel and Hardy in "Nothing But Trouble"
Movie Publicity Showcase Volume 11: Laurel and Hardy in "Blockheads"
Movie Publicity Showcase Volume 12: Laurel and Hardy in "Great Guns"
Movie Publicity Showcase Volume 13: Laurel and Hardy in "The Bohemian Girl"
Movie Publicity Showcase Volume 14: Laurel and Hardy in "A-Haunting We Will Go"
Movie Publicity Showcase Volume 15: Laurel and Hardy in "Jitterbugs"
Laurel and Hardy: The Lobby Cards – A Classic Collection (in Color)
Hal Roach's Rascals: The Our Gang Comedies – A Classic Collection (in Color)

The Movie Publicity Showcase series places movies into their historical "first run" context, utilizing original press material from the time of their release, and subsequent theatrical revivals. Read about your favorite stars as they were during the day of the movie's initial release. See how creative theater managers could draw in an audience when movie exhibition was an art form. Step back into time and see what movie fans of that day experienced when going to the movies!

CPSIA information can be obtained at www.ICGtesting.com
Printed in the USA
LVIW01n1501080818
586367LV00016B/147